Benidorm Travel Guide 2025

BENIDORM TRAVEL GUIDE 2025

Exploring the Beaches, Culture, Nightlife, and Outdoor Activities of Spain's Costa Blanca Jewel.

LEONARD J. LINDSEY

Benidorm Travel Guide 2025

All right reserved. No part of this publication should be reproduced, distributed, or transmitted in any form or by any means, including photocopying, recording, or other electronic or mechanical methods, without the prior written permission of the publisher, except in the case of brief quotations embodied in critical reviews and certain other noncommercial uses permitted by copyright law.

Copyright@ Leonard J. Lindsey, 2024.

Benidorm Travel Guide 2025

Table of Contents

Chapter 1 5
   Introduction to Benidorm: Essential Details to Know 5
   Topography, Culture, and Population 9
Chapter 2 14
   How to Plan Your Trip to Benidorm 14
Chapter 3 22
   Ideal Seasons of the Year to Visit Benidorm 22
   Things to Pack for Your Journey to Benidorm 29
Chapter 4 36
   Accommodation Options in Benidorm 36
   Transportation Options for Tourists 49
Chapter 5 56
   Popular Tourist Attractions in Benidorm 56
   Historical Sites and Monuments 62
   Outdoor Activities for Tourists 68
Chapter 6 76
   Healthy Foods for Tourists in Benidorm 76
   Popular Restaurants for Tourists in Benidorm 83
Chapter 7 91
   Local Crafts and Souvenirs 91

Popular Shopping Centers for Tourists 97
Chapter 8 103
Nightlife Activities in Benidorm for Tourists 103
Chapter 9 110
Itinerary Plan for Tourists in Benidorm............. 110
Common Mistakes Tourists Should Avoid 116

Chapter 1

Introduction to Benidorm: Essential Details to Know

One of Europe's most famous beach resorts is Benidorm, which is situated on the eastern Mediterranean coast of Spain. Over the last several decades, Benidorm has evolved from a sleepy fishing hamlet into a thriving tourist destination, known for its breathtaking beaches, skyline of high-rise buildings, and exciting nightlife. It is often called the "Manhattan of Spain" because of its imposing structures and contemporary ambiance.

With a population of around 75,000, Benidorm is a popular destination for families and partygoers, drawing millions of tourists annually from all over the globe, particularly from the UK and Europe.

The climate

Benidorm's climate is Mediterranean, with around 300 days of sunlight each year. The hot, dry summers are ideal for beachgoers, while the mild winters make it a year-round destination for sun worshippers.

Benidorm Travel Guide 2025

Beaches

Benidorm is well-known for its immaculate beaches. The city's coastline is home to the two major beaches, Levante and Poniente, which have golden sand and crystal-clear seas. While Poniente Beach is more laid-back and ideal for families or those seeking peace and quiet, Levante Beach is well-known for its vibrant environment, water sports, and beach bars.

Blending Cultures

Modern towers contrast with Benidorm's quaint Old Town (Casco Antiguo), creating a blend of the old and the new. The Old Town offers a window into the city's history with its winding lanes, authentic Spanish buildings, neighborhood stores, and eateries. On the other hand, Benidorm's contemporary area is teeming with bars, foreign eateries, and a bustling entertainment district.

Nightlife

With more than 1,000 pubs and 200 clubs, Benidorm is regarded as the nightlife capital of Europe. From all-night discos and beach parties to karaoke bars and Irish pubs, its vibrant environment accommodates a wide range of preferences.

Tourist Destinations

Benidorm has several activities in addition to beaches, such as Aqualandia, one of Europe's biggest water parks, and Terra Mitica, a theme park featuring exhilarating rides. At the marine and animal park Mundomar, guests may get up close and personal with sea lions, dolphins, and other creatures. Hiking in the adjacent Sierra Helada Natural Park and boat excursions to Benidorm Island are well-liked leisure pursuits.

19 Amazing Benidorm Facts Travelers Should Know

- Benidorm, the biggest stag and hen party destination in Europe, is the best place to have a memorable pre-wedding celebration.
- The first city in Spain to permit bikinis on the beach was Benidorm, which was made possible by a progressive mayor in the 1950s.
- More British than Spanish? Particularly in British bars and clubs, you may sometimes hear more English than Spanish.
- There are over thirty LGBTQ+-friendly establishments in Benidorm's gay hamlet, which also holds the yearly Benidorm Pride Festival.
- Benidorm was formerly a fishing community, although it wasn't one as many people think. Its

Benidorm Travel Guide 2025

- fisherman were renowned for their deep-sea expertise.
- With more than 1,000 bars, Benidorm has one of Spain's largest concentrations of bars.
- Cheap beverages abound: 2-for-1 cocktail specials are available almost everywhere.
- Fish are raining! There have been days when fish have showered down from the sky during storms, according to local tales.
- British retirees are drawn to Benidorm because of its sunny climate and reasonably priced way of life.
- Be mindful of segways! Segways are a common method to get about the city, and sometimes they go past at quite high speeds.
- Because of its tall skyline, Benidorm is often compared to New York City, which gives it the odd moniker "Beni-york."
- Because of the large number of British visitors, many people speak English well, negating the need for interpreters.
- Benidorm TV Show: The town is so well-known that it even has its British television show, which is appropriately called Benidorm.
- More sunny days than the UK: Benidorm receives almost twice as many hours of sunlight as London!

- Off the coast of Benidorm, there is a peculiar custom of mailing postcards from a submerged mailbox.
- In the sun, you can ski! Under the Spanish heat, you can ski on the rides at Terra Mitica Theme Park.
- A city without shadows: The beach is always bright because of the city's distinctive design, which prevents any building shadows from obstructing the light.
- Benidorm's "tapas": The Old Town of Benidorm has a tapas path where you may try little treats at reasonable costs.
- Some party streets are known as the "sticky floors" because late-night revelers often drop beverages while dancing there!

Topography, Culture, and Population

Benidorm's topography

Located in the Alicante province of the Valencia autonomous community, Benidorm lies tucked away on Spain's east coast. It has a superb coastline position with large lengths of sandy beaches and warm seas since it is situated on the western side of the Mediterranean Sea. A dramatic contrast between the shore and the untamed interior is produced by the majestic background of the

Benidorm Travel Guide 2025

Puig Campana peak to the west and the Sierra Nevada mountains to the northeast.

The geography of Benidorm greatly adds to its allure. The neighboring mountains provide great chances for hiking and other outdoor pursuits, and the mostly level coastline region makes it simple for visitors to explore on foot. With its striking cliffs and Mediterranean vegetation, the Sierra Helada Natural Park is a well-liked location for nature lovers and provides breathtaking views of the coastline.

The city is well known for its skyline, which is sometimes referred to as "The Manhattan of the Mediterranean" because of the sheer volume of tall structures. The flat coastal plain is dominated by these contemporary buildings, which distinguish Benidorm from other seaside cities in Spain. Its vertical growth-focused urban design made it possible to maximize the amount of space available for lodging and motels, particularly close to the beach.

People living in Benidorm

There are around 75,000 people living in Benidorm, however, this number rises sharply during the tourist season. With more than 10 million people annually, it is one of Spain's most visited locations. The UK is the country from which the most visitors go, followed by Germany, the Netherlands, and Spain.

Because of the city's global appeal, its populace is quite diverse. Due to its good environment and laid-back culture, Benidorm has a sizable expat population, with many British and other European nationalities opting to live there year-round. The population may more than treble during the busiest travel season when short-term tourists outnumber locals. The city's character has changed as a result of this tourist inflow, and it now mostly welcomes foreign guests.

The permanent population of Benidorm is comparatively elderly, and many retirees choose the city because of its sunny climate, reasonably priced housing, and active social scene. But this is counterbalanced by the city's youthful and vibrant vibe, especially in the entertainment and nightlife areas, which draw tourists of all ages.

The Benidorm culture
The culture of Benidorm is a distinctive fusion of contemporary, tourism-driven influences and classic Spanish traditions. Originally a little fishing community, the city is now well-known for its beaches, entertainment, and foreign visitors. This transition has contributed to the creation of a cosmopolitan environment, where British,

Irish, and other European cultural influences are abundantly noticeable.

Numerous festivals are held throughout the city, fusing foreign and local customs. One of the most well-known is Benidorm's Pride Festival, which draws thousands of tourists from all over Europe for a week-long celebration of LGBTQ+ culture. The city also hosts traditional Spanish celebrations including Semana Santa (Holy Week), Las Fallas, and Fiestas Mayores Patronales, which provide a window into its Spanish heritage via folk music, religious processions, and fireworks.

With a variety of different cuisines easily accessible, Benidorm's culinary culture reflects its touristic background. In addition to conventional Spanish tapas restaurants, visitors may discover British pubs that serve fish and chips. In contrast to the city's more contemporary, tourist-focused neighborhoods, the Old Town's winding lanes, neighborhood restaurants, and craft stores provide a more genuine taste of Spanish culture.

Since tourism accounts for a big portion of the local economy, welcoming tourists is fundamental to the culture. There is a ton of entertainment available to travelers, including live concerts, musical acts, and themed events. But even with its state-of-the-art tourist facilities, Benidorm manages to hold onto its authentic

Spanish character, particularly in the Old Town and during cultural events.

To sum up, Benidorm's geography, demographics, and culture all show how the city has been greatly influenced by its natural beauty and the needs of foreign tourists. Benidorm is still one of Spain's most visited tourist attractions because of its distinctive skyline, Mediterranean beaches, multicultural population, and fusion of contemporary and traditional elements.

Chapter 2

How to Plan Your Trip to Benidorm

One of Europe's most popular tourist attractions, Benidorm is situated in the Costa Blanca area of Spain's Mediterranean coast and is well-known for its sandy beaches, exciting nightlife, and breathtaking skyline. Planning a vacation to Benidorm guarantees that you get the most out of this fascinating location, regardless of your travel goals—leisure, adventure, or dynamic city life.

1. Select the Ideal Time to Go

The kind of experience you're seeking, however, will determine the ideal time to go.

High season (June to August): This is the ideal time to visit if you want a thriving nightlife, endless beach days, and exciting events. Remember that this is when the cost of lodging peaks.

Shoulder seasons (April to May and September to October): These months provide the ideal balance if you'd rather avoid crowds and have a little lower temperatures.

Low season (November to March): Winter is the calmest season, perfect for people looking for a more tranquil retreat, even if it's moderate (10°C to 18°C/50°F to 64°F).

2. Establish a Budget

Where you stay, how you travel, and what activities you may engage in will all be greatly influenced by your budget. Benidorm offers accommodations for all price ranges, from luxury vacationers to those seeking a more affordable getaway.

Cost of lodging: Benidorm offers a wide range of hotels, from five-star resorts to inexpensive hostels. While luxury hotels like the Melia Villaitana or Asia Gardens Hotel & Thai Spa may cost more than €200 per night at the busiest times of the year, you can find reasonably priced 3-star hotels for as little as €50 per night.

Entertainment and dining: It's not too expensive to eat out in Benidorm. While more expensive eating alternatives may cost €30 to €50 per person, local eateries provide menus del día (set lunches) for as low as €10. There are several bars, clubs, and live performances; the cost of admission and beverages varies by location.

Excursions and attractions: Water sports, boat excursions, day trips, and theme parks like Terra Mitica or Aqualandia

Benidorm Travel Guide 2025

will raise your total spending limit. You may often save money by making prior reservations and planning ahead.

3. Reserve lodging in the appropriate area.

Three primary sections make up Benidorm, and each one offers a unique experience:

If you want to be right in the middle of the activity, Levante Beach (Playa de Levante) is the place to be. Because of its closeness to the exciting ni toghtlife, it is well-liked by younger travelers and party animals. Modern, high-rise hotels with views of the beach are typical here.

Poniente Beach (Playa de Poniente): This beach has a more laid-back vibe if you want a more sedate vacation. Families and retirees like the region, and the beach is less congested than Levante. This area is home to several high-end hotels that provide a more opulent experience.

Old Town (Casco Antiguo): This quaint neighborhood, with its winding streets, traditional tapas restaurants, and neighborhood stores, is ideal for those looking for a more genuine Spanish experience. Although it's not as busy as the seaside neighborhoods, you can still stroll to the beach.

Benidorm Travel Guide 2025

Think about whether you want quick access to the beach, the nightlife, or historical sites when making your hotel reservation, and be sure to book in advance, particularly if you're going during a busy time of year.

4. Make a Transportation Plan

Alicante Airport (ALC), the nearest international airport, is just 60 kilometers (37 miles) away, making travel to Benidorm very simple. The city may be reached by several modes of transportation:

Airport transportation options from Alicante Airport to Benidorm include taxis, shuttle buses, and private transport. Prices vary from €6 for a shared shuttle to €80 for a private service, and the trip takes around 45 minutes.

Car rentals: If you want to go to the neighboring mountains, Altea, or Guadalupe, renting a car is a great choice. The roads are simple to traverse, and the airport is home to car rental firms.

Public transportation: Buses and trams link Benidorm to neighboring cities like Valencia and Alicante. With lines linking all of the city's main attractions and beaches, the buses are reasonably priced.

Benidorm Travel Guide 2025

Walking around Benidorm is simple once you're there, particularly along the promenades that run down the coastline. For quick excursions, you may also hire a bike or take a cab.

5. Examine the Best Activities and Attractions

From exciting nightlife to family-friendly activities, Benidorm has plenty to offer everyone.

Beaches: Levante and Poniente, the city's two major beaches, are popular destinations. Both have golden beaches and a wide variety of water activities, such as paddleboarding, jet skiing, and parasailing. Go to Mal Pas Beach or Cala Tio Ximo, which are both close by, if you want something more private.

Water parks and theme parks: Terra Mitica is a theme park with thrilling rides and roller coasters that are ideal for thrill-seekers and families. While Mundomar is a marine animal park including dolphin and sea lion performances, Aqualandia is one of the biggest water parks in Europe, featuring pools and slides for all ages.

Explore the quaint Old Town (Casco Antiguo), which is home to cobblestone streets, whitewashed houses, and traditional stores. See the picturesque Mirador del

Benidorm Travel Guide 2025

Castillo, which provides sweeping views of the Mediterranean.

Nightlife: With more than 1,000 pubs and 200 clubs, Benidorm has a famous nightlife. There is something for everyone in Benidorm's nightlife scene, whether you're searching for a quiet drink, live music, or an all-night party.

Outdoor adventures: The natural surroundings of Benidorm are ideal for hiking, mountain biking, and visiting nature reserves like Sierra Helada for people looking for outdoor activities.

6. Make a packing list.

A pleasant and pleasurable trip depends on packing the appropriate things. Here are a few necessities:

Summer essentials: To shield oneself from the intense Mediterranean heat, bring light clothes, beach towels, swimwear, sunscreen, sunglasses, and a hat if you're going in the summer.

Comfortable clothes and walking shoes are vital since Benidorm is a laid-back place.

Evening attire: If you want to dine at posh restaurants or visit clubs, pack some smart-casual attire since many of them have a more formal dress code.

Hiking equipment: Bring proper boots and a lightweight jacket for higher elevations if you want to visit the neighboring mountains or natural parks.

7. Keep yourself safe and be ready.

Even though Benidorm is a usually safe place to visit, it's wise to be cautious:

Safety and health: Ensure that your trip insurance includes emergency medical coverage. Carry a European Health Insurance Card (EHIC) if you are a citizen of the European Union.

Benidorm is a tourist destination, yet it's still vital to observe local rules and decorum. On the beach, bikinis are OK, but not in stores or dining establishments. Although there is a vibrant nightlife, inappropriate conduct may result in penalties and public intoxication is discouraged.

Watch out for valuables: As with any well-known tourist location, petty theft may occur in crowded places, so be sure to keep your possessions safe, particularly on the beach and in areas with a lot of nightlife.

Benidorm Travel Guide 2025

In conclusion, careful preparation is essential for a successful trip to Benidorm, regardless of your preferences for exciting evenings out, leisurely family vacations, or sun-drenched beach days. You're certain to have a memorable stay in this energetic Spanish resort town if you plan, spend appropriately, reserve the ideal lodging, and take advantage of all the city has to offer.

Chapter 3

Ideal Seasons of the Year to Visit Benidorm

A year-round vacation spot with a Mediterranean temperature, Benidorm is a bustling beach resort on Spain's Costa Blanca that draws a diverse array of visitors. Selecting the appropriate season may significantly impact your trip, regardless of whether you are traveling for its famous beaches, exciting nightlife, or scenic beauty.

In order to help you organize your vacation around the things that are most important to you, this guide examines the best times to visit Benidorm based on weather, activities, people, and affordability.

1. Spring: March to May.

Why Spring Is the Best Season:

The weather is ideal for outdoor activities and tourism since it is mild, with temperatures ranging from 15°C (59°F) in March to around 25°C (77°F) in May. Although it may still be a little cold for swimming until late May, the water starts to warm up.

Advantages of Springtime Travel:

Mild Weather: Spring is a terrific time of year for outdoor activities because of the pleasant daytime temperatures and the chilly nights. Without the scorching summer heat, you may trek the trails, visit the Sierra Helada Natural Park, or take leisurely walks along the promenades along the shore.

Fewer Crowds: Because there are fewer visitors in the spring than in the summer, you may enjoy the beaches, dining options, and attractions with fewer people vying for your attention and shorter wait times.

Reduced Costs: Because it's the shoulder season, airfare and lodging are often less expensive, making it the perfect time of year for tourists on a tight budget.

Festivals: Several spring festivals are held in Benidorm, including the Fallas Festival in March, which includes effigy burning, fireworks, and traditional parades. With religious processions and street performances all around the area, April's Easter Week (Semana Santa) festivities provide a distinctive cultural experience.

Considerations:

Sea Temperature: If swimming is a top goal, go later in the season even if the air temperature is moderate. The sea may still be cold in early spring.

2. Summer: June to August.

Why Summer Is the Best Season:

Summer is the prime tourism season in Benidorm, luring people from throughout Europe seeking sun, sea, and sand. With warm nights and long days, temperatures may reach 30°C (86°F) and more, making them ideal for beach holidays. Family vacationers, younger travelers, and those looking for a vibrant nightlife are especially drawn to this time of year.

Advantages of Summer Travel:

Beach Weather: For beach enthusiasts, summer is the best time of year. With pristine seas, plenty of sunlight, and a variety of water activities available, such as jet-skiing, parasailing, and paddleboarding, the beaches of Levante and Poniente are at their finest.

Bright Nightlife: Benidorm is known for its vibrant nightlife, which is at its peak in the summer. Younger people are drawn to bars, nightclubs, and beach parties because they maintain a high level of excitement. Late summer also sees the renowned Benidorm Pride Festival, which offers a vibrant celebration of LGBTQ+ culture.

Family-Friendly Attractions: With theme parks like Terra Mitica and water parks like Aqualandia providing entertainment for all ages, summer is a fantastic season for families. Because of the mild weather, outdoor attractions are always open and running.

Considerations:

Crowds: Because summer is the biggest season, be prepared for packed beaches, lengthy lineups at tourist destinations, and hotels that are completely booked. To guarantee your place, you must reserve your flights, lodging, and activities well in advance.

Expensive: Summertime travel surges drive up costs for everything from lodging and flights to food and entertainment. Be ready for increased expenses if you're on a tight budget, or start looking for sales early.

Heat: Particularly in July and August, the heat may be quite high. Although ideal for beach days, it may not be as pleasant for trekking or touring during the hottest parts of the day. Wear sunblock, drink plenty of water, and take rests in shady spots.

3. Fall: September to November

Why Autumn Is the Best Season:

Another great time to visit Benidorm is in the fall when it's warmer and less crowded. While October and November have milder temperatures, ranging from 18°C to 24°C (64°F to 75°F), September continues to be hot, with highs of around 27°C (81°F).

Advantages of Fall Travel:

Pleasant Weather: Although it doesn't become as hot as it does in the summer, early fall is still pleasant enough to enjoy outdoor activities and the beach.

Fewer Tourists: The crowds lessen when the peak season comes to an end, making it simpler to secure a spot on the beach and take in the calmer ambiance. There is less crowding at restaurants and attractions, making for a more relaxed experience.

Budget-Friendly Travel: Similar to spring, fall is a shoulder season, which means that airfare and lodging are often less expensive than during the summer. Deals on hotels are available now, particularly if you make last-minute reservations.

Events & Festivals: Benidorm honors the town's patron saints with a week-long celebration called the Fiestas Mayores Patronales every November. The celebration gives guests a sense of the local way of life via religious processions, music, and amazing fireworks displays.

Considerations:

Shorter Days: The days become shorter as fall goes on, and the weather might change more suddenly, particularly in late October and early November. Even if it's still nice, you could sometimes get rain or have chilly nights.

4. Winter: December to February

The Benefits of Winter:

During Europe's colder months, Benidorm is a perfect getaway for anyone looking for sunlight and nice weather because of its moderate winters. The typical daytime temperature is between 15°C and 20°C (59°F and 68°F), with colder evening temperatures.

Advantages of Winter Travel:

Benidorm's winters are moderate enough to enjoy outdoor activities like hiking, touring the Old Town, or strolling along the seaside promenades, even if it's not beach weather. With so many golf courses close by, it's also ideal for golfers.

No Crowds: Since fewer people visit in the winter, you may have a quiet, uncrowded experience. Beaches are peaceful and great for walks, but they are not the best places to sunbathe. A more laid-back pace of life is offered by the less crowded restaurants, shopping, and attractions.

Reasonably priced: The best time to visit Benidorm is during the winter. It's a great time for long-term stays or budget-conscious tourists, especially seniors wishing to avoid colder regions since flights and lodging are at their lowest.

Festive Celebrations: Throughout December, Benidorm organizes several seasonal activities, including New Year's Eve festivities, Christmas lights, and festive markets. For winter tourists, Spanish customs like the Three Kings Parade in early January provide a distinctive cultural experience.

Considerations:

Cooler Weather: Although winter days are pleasant, nighttime lows may reach around 8°C (46°F), so bring warm clothing. It's perfect for leisurely walks and outdoor sightseeing, but not for swimming or tanning.

Limited Beach Activities: Winter is not the ideal season to come if you value beach time. There may be fewer water sports available and a reduction in the hours of many beachside cafés and restaurants.

Things to Pack for Your Journey to Benidorm

It's important to pack carefully before traveling to Benidorm, a well-known Spanish vacation city on the Mediterranean coast. Benidorm provides a wide range of activities, including sunny beaches, lively nightlife, and picturesque hiking routes. Being organized is essential for a great holiday. Whether you're traveling in the sweltering summer or the milder off-season, packing well guarantees a relaxing and pleasurable stay.

The necessary goods to pack for various activities, weather situations, and travel preferences are outlined in this article. Here is a thorough list of things to bring for your vacation to Benidorm, including gadgets, beachwear, and travel papers.

1. Clothing Essentials

Benidorm Travel Guide 2025

Benidorm has scorching summers and mild winters due to its Mediterranean environment. The season you're visiting will have a big impact on what you wear, but there are several essentials that you should always carry.

Lightweight Clothes: Bring light, breathable materials like cotton and linen since summer temperatures may get to 30°C (86°F). Light skirts, shorts, tank tops, and t-shirts are ideal for remaining cool throughout the day.

Swimwear: You should bring many swimsuits because of the stunning beaches, such as Playa de Levante and Playa de Poniente. When you transition from the beach to neighboring eateries, think about packing a sarong or cover-up.

Evening Wear: Benidorm is renowned for its vibrant nightlife, with clubs, pubs, and eateries staying open late. Bring something a little more fashionable for nights out, such as a good blouse, fitted shorts, or a smart casual outfit. Bring a lightweight jacket or scarf since the sea wind may make nights cold even in the hottest months.

Wear comfortable shoes since you'll probably be walking a lot in Benidorm, whether it's around the Old Town, along the promenades, or into the Sierra Helada Natural

Park. In addition to flip-flops or water shoes for the beach, bring comfortable walking shoes or sandals.

Layers for Colder Seasons: Pack layers like light sweaters or a jacket if you're traveling in the winter or other colder months. The temperature is nice throughout the day, but in December and January, it might dip to around 8°C (46°F) at night.

2. Beach Equipment

Since Benidorm's beaches are a major draw, having the appropriate equipment can improve your beach experience.

Beach Towel: Although some hotels or beach clubs provide towels, it's a good idea to pack your quick-drying towel, particularly if you want to spend a lot of time on the sand or beach hopping.

Sun Protection: It's crucial to bring sun protection since the Mediterranean sun may be quite strong. Bring a wide-brimmed hat, UV-blocking sunglasses, and sunscreen with a high SPF. If you want to spend a lot of time at the beach, a beach tent or sun umbrella might also be helpful for additional shade.

Reusable Water Bottle: It's important to stay hydrated, particularly during the summer. When going to the beach or engaging in outdoor activities, remember to pack a reusable water bottle. There are drinking water faucets in several Benidorm tourist sites, making it simple to refill your bottle.

Beach Bag: A roomy beach bag is ideal for holding all of your beach necessities, such as a good book, sunscreen, snacks, and a towel. Because sand likes to linger around, choose one that is lightweight and simple to clean.

3. Currency and Travel Documents

A pleasant trip depends on having the right paperwork and being financially prepared.

Identity and Passport: Make sure your passport is valid for the whole journey, and carry a backup copy. It may be sufficient to have a national ID card if you are traveling from inside the EU.

Travel Insurance: Having travel insurance is strongly advised since accidents or unforeseen circumstances might occur. Keep your emergency contact information and insurance policy data close to hand.

Cash and Credit Cards: Although most establishments in Benidorm take credit and debit cards, it's a good idea to keep cash on hand, particularly for modest purchases like market shopping or drinks at beach bars. The native currency is euros (€), and there are several ATMs.

Travel Schedule and Reservations: Make sure you have copies of your travel schedule, hotel bookings, and any attraction or tour tickets. Even if a lot of things are digital, having paper versions on hand might be helpful in case your phone dies or you are unable to access the internet.

4. Health and Toiletries Essential

Although many products are accessible at the local stores in Benidorm, it's always a good idea to pack your favorite toiletries and health supplies.

Basic Toiletries: Bring whatever you need on a regular basis, such as your toothbrush, toothpaste, shampoo, conditioner, and deodorant. The majority of hotels provide toiletries, although they may not be the brands or varieties you want.

First Aid Kit: It's crucial to have a compact first aid kit that includes bandages, antiseptic wipes, painkillers, and any prescription drugs you may have. Think about bringing bug repellent or blister pads if you want to hike or spend a lot of time outside.

Wipes and hand sanitizer are particularly helpful for last-minute cleanups when traveling, as well as for usage before meals or on public transportation.

Prescription Drugs: Make sure to pack enough of any prescription drugs you may be taking for the length of your trip, as well as a copy of your prescription. Basic over-the-counter medications such as motion sickness pills, antihistamines, and anti-diarrheal tablets are also beneficial.

5. Accessories and Electronics
Having the appropriate gadgets with you makes it simpler to stay in touch and take pictures.

Smartphone and Charger: You'll probably use your smartphone for reservations, navigation, and communication. Remember to bring along a charger and, if required, a Spanish outlet adaptor (Spain utilizes Type C and F plugs with a 230V supply).

Camera: From its beaches to the neighboring mountains, Benidorm provides breathtaking vistas. To capture these moments, a camera—or a smartphone with an excellent camera—is necessary. If necessary, bring additional batteries or memory cards.

Portable Power Bank: A portable power bank can keep your gadgets charged while you're out exploring all day long, preventing you from running out of juice while snapping pictures or navigating.

Earbuds or headphones: These are helpful for listening to podcasts or music on buses, airplanes, or when relaxing on the beach.

Depending on the season, packing for Benidorm involves a combination of beach necessities, travel papers, and seasonally suitable apparel. You may concentrate on enjoying your vacation in this stunning Mediterranean location without worrying about what you've left behind if you plan ahead and pack carefully.

Chapter 4

Accommodation Options in Benidorm

Benidorm is one of Spain's most well-known tourist attractions, with magnificent Mediterranean beaches, a busy nightlife, and a diverse range of hotel alternatives to accommodate all types of travelers. If you're searching for a luxurious beachfront hotel, a family-friendly resort, or a low-cost choice, Benidorm provides something for everyone. Let's look at 10 of the best hotels in Benidorm, including their locations, facilities, and pricing ranges, to help you discover the ideal place to stay during your visit.

1. Hotel Don Pancho (Adult Only)

- Address: Avenida del Mediterráneo 39, 03503 Benidorm, Spain.
- Price range: €100 to €300 per night.

Hotel Don Pancho is an adults-only establishment, perfect for those seeking a quiet and serene stay. It is about a two-minute walk from Levante Beach and has contemporary rooms with attractive décor. The hotel has a heated outdoor pool, a Mediterranean restaurant, a fitness facility, and a lounge bar.

Ideal for couples and adults looking for peace while yet being close to nightlife.

2. Asian Gardens Hotel and Thai Spa

- Price range: €200 to €500 per night.

If you want to have an exotic and exquisite experience, Asia Gardens Hotel & Thai Spa offers a one-of-a-kind Asian-inspired getaway. This 5-star hotel is nestled in tropical grounds and has numerous swimming pools, some of which are heated, a Thai spa, and beautiful rooms furnished with Asian themes. The hotel is ideal for individuals who wish to relax in a peaceful environment while being near Benidorm's major attractions.

Ideal for: Luxurious tourists seeking leisure and spa services.

3. Hotel Helios Benidorm

- Address: Avenida Filipinas 12, 03503 Benidorm, Spain.
- Price range: €80 to €200 per night.

Hotel Helios Benidorm, located within a short walk from Levante Beach, is a family-friendly hotel with large rooms and contemporary conveniences. The hotel has a huge outdoor pool, a children's pool, and a health center with a sauna and gym. It also offers a buffet restaurant that serves a range of foreign and Spanish cuisine, as well as daily entertainment for customers of any age.

Ideal for: Families and tourists seeking comfort and amusement.

4. Villa Venecia Hotel - Boutique Gourmet

- Address: Plaza San Jaime 1, 03500 Benidorm, Spain.
- Price range: €250–€600 per night.

Villa Venecia, a 5-star boutique hotel set on a cliff overlooking Benidorm's beaches, is ideal for visitors searching for a luxurious experience. This hotel's deluxe rooms include floor-to-ceiling windows with stunning views of the Mediterranean Sea. It also has a gourmet restaurant, a rooftop patio with a hot tub, and personalized services such as in-room massages.

Best suited for: Couples and visitors seeking luxury and breathtaking vistas.

5. Melia Benidorm

Benidorm Travel Guide 2025

- Address: Avenida Severo Ochoa 1, 03503 Benidorm, Spain.
- Price range: €120–€400 per night.

Melia Benidorm is located in a spacious garden and has contemporary accommodations, a huge lagoon-style swimming pool, and a variety of eating choices. This four-star hotel also has a workout center, an indoor pool, and spa facilities. The hotel's position is somewhat away from the main tourist area, making it an excellent alternative for guests seeking a peaceful stay while being near Levante Beach.

Ideal for: Families and visitors seeking a resort-style experience.

6. Hotel RH Corona Del Mar

- Address: Avenida de la Armada Española, 1, 03502 Benidorm, Spain.
- Price range: €90 to €250 per night.

Hotel RH Corona del Mar is situated directly next to Poniente Beach and provides comfortable accommodations with stunning sea views. It has a huge outdoor pool with a water slide, a buffet restaurant, and a spa center with a sauna and heated indoor pool. The hotel also offers entertainment activities for both adults and children.

Best for: Families and beachgoers seeking a handy location.

7. Magic Natura Resort

- Price range: €150 to €400 per night (all-inclusive).

Magic Natura Resort is a one-of-a-kind family resort situated near Terra Natura Zoo and Aqua Natura Water Park. The resort has Balinese-style bungalows with all-inclusive packages that include admission to the waterpark and zoo. This is an excellent alternative for families seeking an exciting and fun-filled holiday.

Best for: Families with children seeking a balance of rest and activity.

8. Sandos Monaco Beach Hotel & Spa

- Price range: €120 to €350 per night (all-inclusive offered)

Sandos Monaco Beach Hotel & Spa is an adults-only, all-inclusive resort near Levante Beach. The hotel has a beautiful spa with a range of treatments, an outdoor pool, and a restaurant that serves Mediterranean cuisine. Its central position makes it ideal for couples looking to enjoy both the beach and the busy nightlife.

Ideal for: Couples and adults seeking an all-inclusive, adults-only getaway.

9. Hotel Servigroup Venus

- Address: Avenida Filipinas 13, 03503 Benidorm, Spain.
- Price range: €70 to €180 per night.

Hotel Servigroup Venus is a three-star hotel that provides excellent value for money. This hotel, located near Levante Beach, is popular with families and budget-conscious guests. It has a huge outdoor pool, a buffet restaurant with show cooking, and activities for children and adults.

Ideal for: Budget-conscious travelers and families.

10. H10, Porto Poniente

- Address: San Pedro 24, 03501 Benidorm, Spain.
- Price range: €150–€400 per night.

H10 Porto Poniente is a relatively new four-star hotel situated on Poniente Beach. It has exquisite, contemporary rooms with sea views, an infinity pool overlooking the beach, and a rooftop bar. The hotel also has a Despacio Spa Centre, where guests may relax with a variety of therapies.

Ideal for: Travelers seeking contemporary luxury and beachside access.

Alternative Accommodation Options

When visiting Benidorm, many travelers may look for alternatives to standard hotels to fit their budgets, interests, and travel types. Alternative lodging alternatives provide more flexibility, frequently resulting in a more customized and genuine experience. Here's a comprehensive directory of alternative lodging options for travelers visiting Benidorm, including vacation rentals, hostels, eco-lodges, and boutique flats.

1. Vacation Rentals (Airbnb, VRBO, and Similar Platforms)
Vacation rentals have emerged as a popular alternative to hotels, with choices ranging from small flats to enormous villas. Platforms like Airbnb and Vrbo provide a variety of lodgings customized to various visitor needs—whether you're traveling alone, with a partner, or with family.

Benefits: Vacation rentals provide additional room and amenities, such as kitchens and laundry facilities, making them perfect for extended vacations. They are frequently less expensive than hotels, particularly for groups, and provide a more "home-like" feel. Some vacation rentals also include unique properties, such as beachfront villas or penthouse apartments with breathtaking views.

Price varies: Depending on the size, location, and time of year, costs may vary from €50 per night for a basic apartment to €500 for a luxury villa during high season.

Where to Find: Popular sites like Airbnb, Vrbo, and Booking.com allow you to filter by price, location, and amenities.

2. Hostels

Hostels are ideal for budget visitors, backpackers, and individuals who enjoy a social environment. Benidorm has a variety of hostels, many of which provide both dormitory-style and private rooms.

Hostels are inexpensive and often centrally situated, making them an excellent choice for exploring Benidorm on foot. They also provide a community atmosphere in which visitors may interact and mingle, frequently via group activities or city tours offered by the hostel.

Dormitory beds may cost as low as €15-€30 per night, although private rooms at hostels can cost between €40 and €80, making them an economical choice for budget-conscious tourists.

Top hostels in Benidorm:

Hostal Boutique Benidorm Blue Beach: This centrally situated hostel has inexpensive private rooms and a warm ambiance, making it perfect for budget tourists.
Hostal la Barraca: Another economical alternative near the beach that offers dormitory-style and private lodgings.

3. Camping & Glamping

Camping and glamping (luxury camping) may be an interesting lodging alternative for nature lovers and outdoor adventurers. Benidorm and the surrounding area include a variety of campsites, some of which provide contemporary facilities.

Benefits: Camping allows you to remain near nature and may be a cost-effective option for those who don't mind skipping some of the amenities of a hotel. Glamping offers a luxurious outdoor experience without compromising comfort, with fully furnished tents, cabins, or bungalows.

Price Range: Standard camping may cost as low as €10-€20 per night for a tent site, while glamping accommodations can cost between €40 and €150 depending on the degree of luxury.

Where to Camp in Benidorm?

Camping Villasol is a popular campground near the city that offers tent pitches and cottages for a more luxurious stay.
Camping Arena Blanca: Another excellent alternative for caravan and glamping accommodations, with access to a swimming pool and a tranquil location.

4. Boutique Apartments and Aparthotel

Boutique apartments and aparthotels are a fashionable and pleasant option for guests who seek the convenience of hotel-like services combined with the extra room and facilities of an apartment. Aparthotels combine apartment-style accommodations with amenities such as cleaning and front desk help, giving guests the best of both worlds.

Benefits: Boutique flats are ideal for guests seeking a more intimate experience. They often have more distinctive designs and a more welcoming environment than regular hotel rooms. Many aparthotels also have kitchens, making them perfect for guests who wish to cook for themselves during their stay.

Price Range: Prices may range from €60 per night for a modest apartment to €250 for luxurious alternatives during peak season.

Best Aparthotels in Benidorm:

Aparthotel La Era Park: This cheap hotel offers apartments with kitchenettes and sea views, making it an excellent alternative for families and couples.
Les Dunes Suites: These new apartments on the seaside provide breathtaking views of the Mediterranean Sea and convenient access to Benidorm's famed Levante Beach.
5. Guesthouses and Bed & Breakfasts
Guesthouses and bed-and-breakfasts (B&Bs) provide a warm and intimate lodging choice in Benidorm, generally managed by locals who give individual service. These lodgings are often smaller in size but provide a warm ambiance with home-cooked meals and cozy rooms.

Benefits: Staying at a guesthouse or bed and breakfast allows travelers to learn about the local culture and obtain insider advice from their hosts. Breakfast is normally provided, and adding a personal touch may enhance the experience.

Price varies: Prices for guest houses normally vary between €50 and €150 per night, depending on location and quality.

Popular guest houses in Benidorm:

Casa Don Juan is a beautiful bed and breakfast in Benidorm's Old Town that offers cheap accommodations and a pleasant environment.
Gastro Hotel RH Canfali: This B&B offers a boutique guesthouse experience with stunning views of the Mediterranean Sea, combining comfort with gourmet eating.

6. Eco-lodges and Sustainable Accommodations

Eco-lodges and sustainable hotels are becoming popular among ecologically aware vacationers. Benidorm and the neighboring surroundings include a few eco-friendly hotel alternatives that promote sustainable methods like renewable energy, water conservation, and environmentally friendly materials.

Benefits: Guests staying at eco-lodges may reduce their environmental impact while still enjoying luxury and nature. Many eco-lodges are situated in more serene, natural settings, providing a pleasant respite from the city's busier tourist attractions.

Price Range: Eco-lodges and sustainable lodgings may cost between €80 and €200 per night, depending on the degree of elegance and amenities offered.

7. Home Exchange and house-sitting

For adventurous and budget-conscious visitors, home swaps and house sitting are alternatives that enable you to stay in someone's home for free or at a minimal cost. These solutions need some preparation and trust, but they provide a one-of-a-kind chance to explore Benidorm through the eyes of a local.

Benefits: Home exchanges and home sitting provide a more authentic experience since you live like a local. They are also very cost-effective since accommodations are either free or greatly discounted.

Price Range: Because most house swaps are based on reciprocity, the cost is often modest, with the exception of any membership fees charged by the platforms that enable these transactions.

Benidorm has a variety of alternative housing alternatives to suit a broad range of interests, from budget travelers and eco-conscious visitors to luxury seekers and adventurous tourists. Whether you like the communal environment of a hostel, the coziness of a boutique apartment, or the immersive experience of staying in a vacation rental, these options offer better value and a more customized stay than typical hotels.

Transportation Options for Tourists

1. Public Bus System (Autobuses Llorente)

Llorente Bus (part of the ALSA company) operates Benidorm's public bus system, which is an efficient and economical means to get about the city. The buses are contemporary, air-conditioned, and offer consistent service to main metropolitan locations as well as neighboring towns like Alicante and Altea.

Common routes:

Route 2 connects Benidorm's Old Town to Levante Beach and residential neighborhoods like La Cala.
Route 3 connects Benidorm's city center with the famed Terra Mítica theme park.

Route 10: One of the principal roads, it links Benidorm to Altea and Albir, two seaside communities north of the city.

Price Range: A single ride inside the city costs around €1.60. If you want to use the bus often, you may buy a rechargeable BonoBus card that provides savings for several journeys. A 10-trip card costs about €9.60, giving it an affordable choice for longer trips.

Buses operate every 10-30 minutes, depending on the route and time of day, with more regular service in the summer.

2. Tram (Tram Metropolitano Alicante)

The TRAM system is a light rail service that links Benidorm to Alicante and other Costa Blanca cities. It's a beautiful and pleasant way to travel, particularly for visitors wishing to explore the area.

Common routes:

Line 1 is the major route between Alicante and Benidorm. The ride lasts roughly 70 minutes and takes you through stunning coastal vistas.

Line 9 connects Benidorm to Denia, another picturesque beach resort north of Benidorm. This is an excellent path for anyone seeking to go beyond Benidorm.

Benidorm Travel Guide 2025

Price Range: A one-way trip from Benidorm to Alicante costs roughly €4.60. Shorter rides between Benidorm and surrounding towns such as Altea or Villajoyosa cost between €1.35 and €2.50.

Trams operate every 30 minutes to an hour, with fewer services on weekends and public holidays. The trams are noted for their timeliness and cleanliness, making them a popular option for visitors.

3. Taxi Services

Taxis are commonly accessible in Benidorm and provide a simple and relatively quick means to move about the city or to surrounding sites, particularly for people traveling in groups or with baggage. Licensed taxis in Benidorm are white with a blue stripe and may be hailed on the street, at authorized taxi ranks, or by phone.

Common routes:

A short journey through the city center, such as from Levante Beach to Benidorm Old Town, usually costs between €5 and €10.
Terra Mítica, Aqualandia, and other local attractions are normally priced between €10 and €15.

Price Range: The standard rate is €4 during the day and €6 at night, with an extra fee of €1 per kilometer. Taxi costs rise somewhat after 9 p.m. and on weekends.

Taxis are readily available throughout the city, particularly in tourist districts such as Rincon de Loix and Benidorm Old Town. Taxi ranks are available in important locations such as Levante Beach, Alicante Airport, and Benidorm Bus Station.

4. Car Rentals

Renting a vehicle is an excellent alternative for those who value freedom and wish to explore the Costa Blanca area beyond Benidorm. Numerous international and local car rental businesses operate in Benidorm, providing a diverse selection of automobiles.

Common routes:

A lovely trip to Guadalest, a charming mountain community located around 25 kilometers from Benidorm. The seaside trip to Denia via the N-332, a scenic road that goes through tiny villages like Altea and Calpe.
Rental fees vary by season and vehicle type. In the off-season, a compact automobile may cost as low as €20-€30 per day, but bigger or luxury vehicles might cost between

€50 and €100. During the peak season, prices might rise by up to 50%.

Parking Fees: Finding parking in Benidorm's city center might be difficult, particularly during peak season. Many hotels provide parking, however, public spaces cost between €2 and €3 per hour, with daily fees ranging from €10 to €20.

5. Bicycle and Scooter Rentals

Benidorm is a bike-friendly city with multiple designated cycle tracks, making bicycles and scooters a fun and environmentally beneficial way to get about. Many rental companies provide reasonable pricing, and electric scooters are becoming more popular among travelers seeking a fast and convenient way to explore.

Common routes:

A popular bicycle route is along the Levante Beach and Poniente Beach promenade, which provides spectacular views of the Mediterranean.
Biking or scootering around Benidorm's Old Town enables visitors to discover its tiny alleyways and colorful atmosphere.

For a more adventurous ride, travel to the Sierra Helada Natural Park, which offers stunning views of Benidorm's cityscape.

Pricing Range:

Bike rentals normally cost between €10 and €15 per day. Electric scooter rentals cost from €20 to €35 per day, depending on the type and length of the rental.

Where to Rent: There are several rental businesses around Levante Beach and Rincon de Loix. Many stores now provide guided bike tours of Benidorm and its neighboring regions.

6. BeniConnect Shuttle Services

Beniconnect is a popular and reasonably priced shuttle service for people arriving at Alicante Airport or traveling between major Costa Blanca locations. It is a shared transportation alternative that connects Benidorm, Alicante, and many other Costa Blanca cities.

Common routes:

Regular shuttle services from Alicante Airport to Benidorm, including stops at famous hotels and tourist attractions.

Beniconnect also serves Albir, Calpe, and Torrevieja, among other locations.

Price Range: A one-way ride from Alicante Airport to Benidorm costs roughly €10-€12 per person, making it an affordable alternative for lone tourists or small parties.

Shuttle services operate throughout the day, scheduled to coincide with airline arrivals and departures at Alicante Airport. Pre-booking is advised, particularly during peak season.

Benidorm has a range of transportation alternatives to accommodate various budgets, interests, and travel plans. Visitors may easily travel the city and explore its surroundings, thanks to the economical public bus and tram systems, as well as the ease of taxis and vehicle rental services. Bicycles and scooters are ideal for eco-friendly guests who want to explore the sites at their leisure, while shuttle services such as Beniconnect provide convenient airport connections.

Chapter 5

Popular Tourist Attractions in Benidorm

Beaches in Benidorm

Benidorm is recognized for its picturesque Mediterranean coastline, which includes some of Spain's best beaches. Benidorm's beaches are popular among visitors due to its crystal-clear waves, smooth golden sands, and diverse range of water activities and services. Whether you want a busy beach experience or a more isolated location to relax, there is something for everyone.

1. Levante Beach (Playa del Levante)

Levante Beach, one of Benidorm's most recognizable beaches, is a 2-kilometer strip of golden sand on the city's east side.

Atmosphere and Activities: Levante Beach is often alive with activities. It is dotted with bars, restaurants, and stores, making it an excellent choice for anyone looking for a bustling beach experience. The beach is ideal for

Benidorm Travel Guide 2025

water sports aficionados, with options such as jet skiing, parasailing, and paddleboarding. The broad promenade is ideal for a leisurely walk, and at night, Levante Beach transforms into a destination for nightlife, with several beach bars open until late.

Facilities at Levante Beach include loungers, parasols, showers, and public bathrooms. There are also lifeguards on duty, so it is a safe choice for families with children.

Accessibility: It is readily accessible from most areas of the city, with various local hotels and public transportation options.

Sunbed and parasol rentals normally cost between €5 and €6 per day.

2. Poniente Beach (Playa Poniente)

Poniente Beach is an excellent alternative to the crowded Levante Beach for those seeking a more quiet and laid-back experience. Poniente Beach, which stretches for nearly three kilometers, is situated on Benidorm's western side.

Poniente Beach is calmer and less busy than Levante Beach, making it excellent for children, couples, and anyone seeking a more peaceful environment. Despite the quieter atmosphere, there is still much to do, from kayaking to beach volleyball. The promenade along Poniente is contemporary and expansive, ideal for a sunset stroll, cycling, or just admiring the scenery.

Poniente, like Levante Beach, has excellent services such as sunbed rentals, restaurants, cafés, and lifeguard stations. It also features specialized sports spaces and wheelchair-accessible zones.

Accessibility: Poniente Beach is readily accessible by foot or public transportation, and it is flanked by hotels and vacation homes.

Sunbed and umbrella rentals, like those in Levante, cost between €5 and €6 per item. Parking places near the beach are also available, with rates ranging from €2 to €3 per hour.

3. Mal Pas Beach (playa del Mal Pas)

Mal Pas Beach is ideal for those seeking a more private and personal beach experience. Mal Pas is a tiny, secluded cove nestled between Levante and Poniente beaches, famed for its crystal-clear waters and serene environment.

Atmosphere and Activities: Mal Pas Beach is calmer than its bigger competitors, providing a serene respite for those seeking to avoid the throng. The calm seas are good for snorkeling and swimming since marine life is more evident in this location. The beach is ideal for couples or lone tourists looking for leisure.

Facilities: Although Mal Pas Beach is smaller, it still has basic services including showers and sun beds. However, amenities are more restricted than at bigger beaches, so bring your food and beverages.

Accessibility: The beach is reached by a series of steps from the Mirador del Castillo, a picturesque overlook with breathtaking views of the coast. Because of its position, Mal Pas is significantly less accessible to persons with mobility impairments.

Sunbed and parasol rentals are available for between €5 and €6. Parking near the old town might be more difficult, so come early or use public transportation.

4. Cala Tio Ximo.

Cala Tio Ximo is a hidden treasure for anyone looking for a unique trip. This little, rocky bay, nestled at the base of the Sierra Helada Natural Park, is a world apart from Benidorm's crowded major beaches.

Cala Tio Ximo provides a more rocky, natural beach experience. It is popular among snorkelers and divers because of its clear waters and rocky bottom, which is home to a diverse range of marine species. The beach is tiny, remote, and underdeveloped, making it ideal for anyone seeking a peaceful retreat surrounded by nature.

This beach has few amenities, so guests should bring their own food, water, and beach equipment. Sunbeds and parasols are not available for hire, so bring your beach mat or towel.

Accessibility: Cala Tio Ximo is a little more difficult to get than other beaches, needing a short stroll down a trail. The beach's remote position also means fewer people, making it a perfect destination for those seeking a more adventurous experience.

Price Range: Because there are no rentals available, this beach is virtually free, while parking in surrounding neighborhoods may cost between €2-€4 an hour.

5. Cala Almadraba

Cala Almadraba, another gorgeous and tranquil bay near the Sierra Helada cliffs, is a favorite snorkeling and swimming area. It is one of Benidorm's more natural beaches, with less development and a focus on the surrounding nature.

Cala Almadraba is ideal for wildlife enthusiasts. The crystal-clear waters and rocky surroundings are great for snorkeling and diving. It is significantly calmer than Levante and Poniente, providing a peaceful setting for relaxing and swimming.

Similar to Cala Tio Ximo, amenities are limited, with no sunbeds or parasols accessible. There are no restaurants or bars nearby, so pack a picnic and carry plenty of water.

Accessibility: The beach is accessible by a route from the Sierra Helada Natural Park. It's a little more difficult to reach, which adds to its hidden appeal.

Price Range: Cala Almadraba is free to see, although neighboring parking costs €2-€3 an hour.

6. Racó de l'Oix.

Racó de l'Oix, located at the further end of Levante Beach, provides a more relaxing beach experience while being near to the excitement. This region is popular among residents and families owing to its peaceful vibe when compared to downtown Levante.

Racó de l'Oix is ideal for swimming, sunbathing, and admiring the Mediterranean scenery. It is less busy than the main portion of Levante but still provides a variety of sports such as kayaking and paddleboarding.

Facilities include restaurants, cafés, loungers, and umbrellas for hire, as well as public bathrooms and lifeguard posts.

Accessibility: Racó de l'Oix is easily accessible by foot from Levante Beach or by public transportation, making it an ideal alternative for those seeking a more calm beach experience while being near the city's facilities.

Sunbed and parasol rentals, like those in Levante, cost between €5 and €6 per item.

Benidorm's beaches provide something for everyone, from the vibrant and bustling Levante Beach to the peaceful and natural coves of Cala Tio Ximo and Cala Almadraba.

Historical Sites and Monuments

Benidorm, a dynamic coastal city famed for its beaches and nightlife, also has a fascinating history, with various historical landmarks and monuments that provide travelers with an insight into its colorful past. From ancient ruins to medieval constructions, these sights depict Benidorm's transformation from a modest fishing community to a popular tourist resort.

1. Tossal de la Cala

Tossal de la Cala, an old Iberian hamlet on a hill above Poniente Beach, is one of Benidorm's most notable historical sites. This archeological site, dating back to the third century BC, offers a fascinating glimpse into the region's history.

Historical Importance: The Tossal de la Cala was initially utilized as a defense village by the Iberians, as shown by its strategic position along the shoreline. Numerous items, including pottery and tools, have been discovered during excavations, allowing researchers to reconstruct the everyday life of the ancient people. Later, during the Roman Empire, the location was fortified further to guard against invading armies.

What to See: Visitors may explore the ruins of the ancient walls, buildings, and defenses, as well as take in panoramic views of the surrounding shore. The site also has interpretative panels that detail the settlement's history and importance.

The Tossal de la Cala is positioned on a hill near the western end of Poniente Beach, therefore it is readily accessible to guests.

2. Benidorm Old Town (Casco Antiguo).

Benidorm's Old Town, or Casco Antiguo, is a picturesque and historically significant district tucked between the city's more contemporary areas. This district, with its tiny, cobblestoned lanes and typical white-washed cottages, recalls the city's old-world beauty before it became a booming tourist destination.

Historical significance: During Benidorm's early days as a fishing community, the Old Town served as the hub of the city. It has retained most of its historic construction and layout, with some buildings going back hundreds of years. Walking through the Old Town is like taking a step back in time, in sharp contrast to the city's skyscrapers and new buildings.

What to See: San Jaime Church (Iglesia de San Jaime y Santa Ana), an 18th-century church with a stunning blue-tiled dome and interior, and Plaza del Castillo, the site of a historic stronghold that formerly defended the city from pirate assaults, are two must-sees in Old Town. The Balcony of the Mediterranean, situated at the end of the Old Town, is a picturesque vantage that provides breathtaking views of the sea and surrounding surroundings.

The Old Town is readily accessible from both Levante and Poniente beaches since it is located on a short hill between them.

3. Iglesia of San Jaime y Santa Ana.

The San Jaime and Santa Ana Church, situated in the center of Benidorm's Old Town, is one of the city's most significant religious structures. This church was built in the 18th century and is dedicated to Saint James, Benidorm's patron saint.

Architectural Style: The church is a beautiful example of classic Mediterranean architecture, with a blue-tiled dome that is typical of churches in Alicante. Inside, visitors may see the magnificent altar, wonderful religious artwork, and the figure of the Virgin of Sufragio, Benidorm's patron saint.

Religious Significance: The church plays an important part in local religious celebrations, such as the Fiestas Patronales, which take place every November to honor the Virgin of Sufragio. During these festivals, the cathedral serves as the focal point for processions and religious activities, drawing thousands of people.

Benidorm Travel Guide 2025

Location: The church is situated on the Plaza de San Jaime, in the center of Benidorm's Old Town, and is a must-see for those interested in the city's religious heritage.

4. El Mirador del Castillo (The Castle Viewpoint)

El Mirador del Castillo is a historic monument at the pinnacle of the Old Town that provides stunning panoramic views of both the Levante and Poniente beaches. This viewpoint was previously the site of Benidorm's ancient castle, which guarded the city throughout the Middle Ages.

Historical significance: The fortress was erected in the 14th century to defend against pirate assaults, which were widespread in the area at the time. Although the castle was dismantled in the nineteenth century, portions of its original defenses remain, and tourists may view relics of the castle walls.

What to See: The viewpoint, known as the "Balcony of the Mediterranean," provides breathtaking views of the shore and water. It's also a popular site for travelers to snap pictures and admire the scenery. The plaza around the viewpoint is often filled with street performers and merchants, which adds to the vibrant ambiance.

El Mirador del Castillo is located at the end of Old Town, only a short walk from the San Jaime Church and other attractions.

5. Torre Punta del Cavall (Vigía)

Another noteworthy historical landmark in Benidorm is the Torre Punta del Cavall, a watchtower in the Sierra Helada Natural Park. This tower, constructed in the 16th century, was part of a coastal defensive system intended to safeguard the region from pirate invasions.

Historical Role: The watchtower was strategically placed atop a cliff to afford a good view of the surrounding shore. Soldiers stationed in the tower would keep an eye out for oncoming pirate ships and alert adjacent communities to any potential hazards. The tower is one of numerous similar buildings that originally lined the coast of Alicante province.

What to See: Although the tower is not available to the public, tourists may trek to the location and take in the breathtaking views of the Mediterranean Sea and the surrounding terrain. The climb is quite straightforward and lasts around 30 minutes, making it a popular choice for both nature enthusiasts and history aficionados.

The Torre Punta del Cavall is situated in the Sierra Helada Natural Park, only a short drive from Benidorm's downtown.

6. Calle Mayor

Calle Mayor is one of Benidorm's oldest streets, reminding visitors of the city's rich history. This tiny, meandering lane, surrounded by historic Spanish houses, is a favorite tourist destination.

Calle Mayor is situated in the center of the Old Town and has played an important role in Benidorm's history from its inception as a fishing community. The street is lined with ancient structures, including traditional residences and stores that have been handed down through generations.

What to See: Visitors may wander among the charming shops, cafés, and bars that line the street, many of which sell traditional Spanish items and food. It's an excellent location to learn about local culture and history while enjoying the vibrant ambiance of the Old Town.

Outdoor Activities for Tourists

1. Hiking & Walking Trails

Benidorm's terrain has several hiking paths, ranging from easy treks to more difficult excursions. These routes lead you through gorgeous natural parks, steep mountains, and seaside walks with stunning views of the Mediterranean.

Sierra Helada Natural Park: One of the most popular hiking destinations in Benidorm, Sierra Helada (or Serra Gelada in Valencian) offers a variety of paths that go over difficult terrain with breathtaking views of the Mediterranean. The Punta del Cavall route goes to a historic watchtower, whilst the Lighthouse of Albir trail is a more accessible walk with panoramic views.

La Cruz de Benidorm: Another popular hiking site, this route leads to a big cross on a hill overlooking the city. The climb provides stunning views of the coastline, particularly around sunset.

Puig Campana: For more experienced hikers, the hard trek to the summit of Puig Campana, Alicante province's second-highest peak, provides stunning vistas and a satisfying feeling of success. It's a difficult, rocky climb, but the panoramic view of the surrounding region is well worth it.

2. Water Sports

Benidorm's seaside position makes it an ideal place for water sports. Whether you like fast-paced activity or a more calm atmosphere, there is something for everyone.

Jet Skiing: The exhilaration of jet skiing is difficult to match. Several firms in Benidorm rent jet skis and provide guided trips, enabling you to explore the coast while experiencing the adrenaline of the open sea. Prices vary but commonly begin at €80 for a 30-minute session.

Parasailing: For a bird's-eye view of Benidorm, fly over the beaches and get a unique perspective on the city. This sport is accessible on both the Levante and Poniente beaches and normally costs between €50 and €70 per person for a 15-20 minute flight.

Kayaking and paddleboarding provide a more leisurely approach to exploring Benidorm's crystal-clear waters. Many firms provide guided trips around the coast, bringing you to secluded coves and beaches that are otherwise inaccessible. Kayak and paddleboard rentals start from €15 per hour.

3. Snorkeling and Scuba Diving

The Mediterranean's clean, mild seas make Benidorm an ideal location for snorkeling and scuba diving. The underwater environment here is filled with marine life, and various businesses provide guided tours for both novices and experienced divers.

Snorkeling: You don't have to go far from the beach to witness colorful fish and undersea life. The region surrounding Benidorm Island is especially popular for snorkeling, because of its rugged underwater landscape and crystal-clear waters, which allow you can see fish, octopuses, and even rays.

Scuba diving is the ideal method to experience Benidorm's marine life and underwater scenery. Certified divers may explore a variety of diving destinations, including the seas around Benidorm Island and La Llosa, an underwater mountain. For novices, many diving schools offer introductory dives, with pricing often beginning at €60 for a basic dive.

4. Cycling

Whether you're a casual rider looking for a leisurely ride along the coast or a dedicated cyclist searching for a challenge, there are several possibilities.

Coastline Rides: For those looking for a more peaceful cycling experience, Benidorm's coastline routes provide breathtaking vistas and easy terrain. Renting a bike is simple, with several rental outlets around the city providing hourly and daily prices (beginning at roughly €10 per day).

Mountain Biking: For more daring bikers, the hills and mountains around Benidorm provide tough courses with steep climbs and spectacular descents. Mountain biking is popular on the routes of Sierra Helada and Puig Campana.

5. Boat trips

Exploring the shore from the ocean provides a unique viewpoint of Benidorm's natural beauty. There are many boat cruises offered to suit different interests.

Benidorm Island Boat Trip: A short boat journey from the harbor transports you to Benidorm Island, a tiny, deserted island off the coast. Once on the island, you may explore the rocky landscape, dive in the pristine seas, or just admire the scenery. The boat ride usually costs around €15 for adults and €12 for youngsters.

Coastal Cruises: If you want to relax while taking in the scenery, a coastal cruise is an excellent choice. These excursions normally run between one and two hours and take you around Benidorm's lovely beaches and cliffs. Some tours even have glass-bottom boats, so you can explore the undersea environment without getting wet.

Benidorm Travel Guide 2025

6. Theme and Adventure Parks

Benidorm has a multitude of theme parks and adventure parks for families and thrill seekers to enjoy an exciting day out.

Terra Mítica is one of Spain's biggest theme parks, with exciting rides, live concerts, and themed zones based on ancient civilizations such as Egypt, Greece, and Rome.

Aqualandia: If you're traveling in the summer, Aqualandia is the ideal spot to cool off. This water park has a range of water slides, pools, and attractions suitable for all ages. It is one of Europe's biggest water parks, situated close to Benidorm.

Mundomar is a marine and exotic animal park situated near Aqualandia that is popular among wildlife enthusiasts. The park is home to dolphins, sea lions, and a variety of bird species, and it provides daily presentations and participatory activities such as swimming with dolphins.

7. Golfing

Benidorm has various golf courses that cater to both beginners and expert players. The city's warm temperature makes it an attractive golfing destination all year round.

Villaitana Golf, located just outside Benidorm, has two 18-hole courses built by Jack Nicklaus. Green fees normally vary between €50 and €100, depending on the time of year and course.

Las Rejas Open Club: For a more casual golfing experience, Las Rejas has a 9-hole course near the city center. It's an excellent choice for novices or anybody seeking a fast game of golf.

8. Paragliding

Paragliding above Benidorm provides a unique and adrenaline-pumping experience, with breathtaking aerial views of the city and beach. Several firms provide tandem paragliding trips with professional instructors, making it accessible even to first-timers.

Price varies: Prices for paragliding excursions normally vary between €90 and €120, depending on the length and operator.

Benidorm has an astonishing selection of outdoor activities for all types of holidaymakers. There is something for everyone, whether you want to go on an adventure in the mountains, have fun on the sea, or relax on the golf course.

Benidorm Travel Guide 2025

The city's natural beauty and diversified scenery offer the ideal background for outdoor activities, guaranteeing that your trip to Benidorm is full of unforgettable experiences.

Chapter 6

Healthy Foods for Tourists in Benidorm

Benidorm, a major tourist resort on Spain's Costa Blanca, provides not just sun and beaches, but also a diverse culinary experience. Tourists visiting Benidorm may eat a variety of delicacies, from traditional Spanish dishes to other cuisines. Many of these foods are not only tasty but also have many health benefits.

1. Paella

Paella, a popular Spanish dish, developed in the Valencia area, near Benidorm. It's a must-try for travelers in the region. The meal contains rice, saffron, different meats (chicken, rabbit, or shellfish), veggies, and olive oil. There are many types of paella, including seafood, vegetarian, and mixed variants.

Health Benefits:

- Protein-rich: Paella contains plenty of protein, which is necessary for muscle repair and development.

Benidorm Travel Guide 2025

- Antioxidants: Saffron, one of the major components, is high in antioxidants, which help protect the body from oxidative stress and inflammation.
- Fiber: Vegetables such as peas, beans, and tomatoes in paella have a significant quantity of fiber, which aids digestion and improves gut health.

2. Tapas

Benidorm, like most of Spain, is well-known for its tapas, which are tiny, tasty appetizers paired with beverages. Tapas may vary from basic olives or almonds to more sophisticated compositions like Spanish patatas bravas (fried potatoes with spicy sauce), jamón ibérico (Iberian ham), and gambas al ajillo (garlic shrimp).

Health Benefits:

- Healthy fats: Tapas like olives and jamón ibérico include heart-healthy monounsaturated fats that help decrease harmful cholesterol.
- Many tapas recipes feature vegetables like tomatoes, peppers, and spinach, which are high in vitamins A, C, and K.
- Omega-3 fatty acids: Tapas containing seafood, such as garlic shrimp, are high in omega-3 fatty

acids, which are beneficial to brain health and reduce inflammation.

3. Gazpacho

Gazpacho is a chilled tomato soup that is particularly popular in Spain during the hot summer months. It's a pleasant salad composed of tomatoes, cucumbers, bell peppers, onions, garlic, olive oil, and vinegar.

Health Benefits:

- Gazpacho is a hydrating meal owing to the high water content of the tomatoes and cucumbers, making it an excellent choice for remaining cool and refreshed in Benidorm's hot weather.
- Gazpacho is low in calories and fat, making it a good alternative for individuals who want to eat healthily while traveling.
- Tomatoes are abundant in lycopene, a potent antioxidant that helps against heart disease and some cancers.

4. Fideuà

This seafood meal is made with squid, shrimp, and clams and is seasoned with saffron and garlic.

Health Benefits:

- Fideuà's seafood is abundant in protein, which promotes muscular health and metabolism.
- Omega-3 fatty acids: Like many seafood recipes, fideuà has a healthy amount of omega-3 fatty acids, which are beneficial to cardiovascular health.
- Low in saturated fats: Fideuà has less saturated fats than meat-heavy meals, making it a heart-healthy choice for travelers.

5. Churros with chocolate.

For a sweet treat, guests may try churros con chocolate, a classic Spanish delicacy composed of fried dough served with thick, hot chocolate to dip. While churros are not exactly a healthy food, consuming them in moderation may provide some advantages.

Health Benefits:

- Mood booster: The dark chocolate used for dipping is high in flavonoids, which are substances that may promote mood and cognitive performance.

- Churros are a rapid supply of carbs, making them an ideal snack for travelers seeking an energy boost after a day of touring.

6. Arroz a Banda

Arroz a banda is a rice dish similar to paella, but cooked in a fish broth and served with seafood, often prawns and squid. This meal is a Costa Blanca staple, especially Benidorm.

Health Benefits:

- Protein and omega-3s: The seafood in Arroz a banda contains lean protein and heart-healthy omega-3 fatty acids.
- Low-fat option: When compared to other meat-based recipes, arroz a banda is a lighter, lower-fat alternative that is nevertheless full of flavor and nutrition.
- Minerals: Seafood contains minerals such as zinc, iron, and iodine, all of which help with immune function and thyroid health.

7. Cocido

Cocido is a typical Spanish stew prepared with chickpeas, vegetables, and meats such as chorizo, ham, or chicken.

It's a meaty meal that's popular throughout Spain's colder months.

Health Benefits:

- Chickpeas are a high-fiber food that promotes good digestion and decreases cholesterol levels.
- Packed in vitamins and minerals: The veggies used in cocido provide critical vitamins such as vitamin C, vitamin A, and potassium.
- Cocido's meat and beans provide an excellent mix of animal and plant proteins, making it a filling and nutritious meal.

8. Turrón

Turrón is a delicious dessert with certain nutritional advantages because of its natural components.

Health Benefits:

- Turrón's almonds include monounsaturated fats, which are helpful to heart health.
- Honey is high in antioxidants, which may help decrease inflammation and boost the immune system.
- Almonds are a plant-based source of protein.

9. Ensalada Valenciana

Ensalada Valenciana is a pleasant Mediterranean salad composed of tomatoes, onions, olives, and sometimes tuna, drizzled with olive oil and vinegar.

Health Benefits:

- Low in calories: This salad is a light, low-calorie alternative that is ideal for a nutritious supper.
- Healthy fats: The olives and olive oil in the salad include monounsaturated fats, which promote heart health.
- High in vitamins: Tomatoes are high in vitamin C and antioxidants like lycopene, but onions contain quercetin, a flavonoid with anti-inflammatory qualities.

10. Padrón peppers

Pimientos de padrón, little green peppers, are cooked in olive oil and seasoned with salt. They are a famous tapas dish in Benidorm, with a variety of mild and hot peppers.

Health Benefits:

- Peppers have significant levels of antioxidants such as vitamin C and beta-carotene, which help protect cells from harm.
- Low in calories and fat: This meal is a nutritious snack or side dish.

Popular Restaurants for Tourists in Benidorm.

1. La Cava Aragonesa

La Cava Aragonesa, located in the heart of Benidorm's Old Town, is a popular destination for travelers seeking traditional Spanish tapas. The restaurant serves over 40 different tapas, including jamón ibérico, shellfish, and local cheeses. It's the ideal spot to try classic Spanish cuisine, thanks to its lively environment and diverse menu.

Address: Plaza de la Constitución 2, Benidorm
Price range: €15 to €25 per person.

Why tourists love it:

- Authentic Spanish Experience
- An extensive assortment of tapas
- Ideal for groups and sharing platters.

2. Ulia Restaurant

Ulia Restaurant is a must-visit for seafood enthusiasts. Located on Poniente Beach, this restaurant specializes in Mediterranean and seafood specialties, notably paella. Ulia, which has breathtaking views of the sea, combines superb meals with an unrivaled setting. It's an excellent choice for a relaxing lunch or a romantic evening.

Address: Avenida Vicente Llorca Alós 15, Benidorm.
Price range: €30-50 per person.

Why tourists love it:

- Fresh fish and Paella specialties
- Beachfront dining with magnificent views
- Elegant but casual environment

3. Restaurante Belvedere

Restaurant Belvedere, located atop a skyscraper with panoramic views of Benidorm's skyline and the Mediterranean Sea, provides a magnificent dining experience suitable for special occasions. The menu includes a variety of Mediterranean and foreign foods, and the restaurant is noted for its excellent service.

Address: Avenida de Madrid 14, Benidorm.

Price range: €40–€60 per person.

Why tourists love it:

- Stunning views across Benidorm
- High-end, refined environment.
- Ideal for romantic meals and festivities.

4. Two Palms Restaurant

Two Palms is a British-owned restaurant that has grown popular among travelers seeking a substantial, home-cooked supper. It is situated in Benidorm's Old Town and serves a mix of British and Mediterranean dishes. Two Palms, known for its courteous service and warm setting, is ideal for families and individuals looking for familiar cuisine.

Address: Calle de la Palma 30, Benidorm.
Price range: €12 to €20 per person.

Why tourists love it:

- Ideal for British cuisine and comfort meals.
- A friendly, inviting environment
- Reasonably priced lunches with large quantities

5. Amigos Restaurant & Roof Terrace

Another popular destination for Benidorm tourists is Amigos Restaurant and Roof Terrace. It has a diverse menu, including steaks, seafood, and vegetarian alternatives, all in a classy environment. The rooftop patio is ideal for evening meals, with views of the town and a comfortable, intimate ambiance.

Address: Calle de Alicante 14, Benidorm.
Price range: €25 to €35 per person.

Why tourists love it:

- Rooftop seating with spectacular views.
- Modern menu with foreign inspirations.
- Excellent service, polite people.

6. Mediterranean Cuisine El Mesón

El Mesón is the place to go if you want a real taste of Mediterranean food. This restaurant near Levante Beach serves classic Mediterranean food, including fideuà (similar to paella but with noodles) and arroz a banda (rice cooked in fish stock). The restaurant takes pleasure in utilizing fresh, locally sourced food.

Address: Avenida de la Armada Española, 19. Benidorm.
Price range: €25 to €45 per person.

Why tourists love it:

- Specializes in local fish and rice meals.
- Close to the beach.
- Traditional, rustic vibe.

7. The Vagabond

The Vagabond, one of Benidorm's most popular hidden jewels, serves a unique combination of French and Mediterranean food. It's a modest, charming restaurant in the Old Town, and the proprietor, Jean, is well-known for his warmth and personalized service to tourists. The cozy environment is ideal for couples and small groups.

Address: Calle de los Arcos 3, Benidorm.
Price range: €20 to €30 per person.

Why tourists love it:

- The owner provides personalized service and attention.
- Cozy, personal environment.
- A distinct French-Mediterranean fusion food.

8. Duetto Pizzeria & Trattoria

Benidorm Travel Guide 2025

Duetto is a popular Italian restaurant in Benidorm. Duetto, renowned for its wood-fired pizzas and handmade pasta, provides a taste of Italy in the heart of Spain. The restaurant is positioned somewhat away from the tourist districts, giving it a more casual and genuine atmosphere.

Address: Avenida de Montecarlo 4, Benidorm.
Price range: €10 to €20 per person.

Why tourists love it:

- Authentic Italian Cuisine
- Affordable prices
- Relaxed, easygoing atmosphere

9. Casa Toni

Casa Toni, a famous destination for traditional Spanish cuisine, is noted for its welcoming environment and delicious food. It is located in the Old Town and provides a range of Spanish favorites such as paella, shellfish, and grilled meats. The restaurant offers a rustic appeal and substantial quantities, making it popular among families and large parties.

Address: Avenida de Europa 8, Benidorm.
Price range: €15 to €35 per person.

Why tourists love it:

- Excellent range of classic Spanish meals.
- Family-friendly environment
- Generous servings

10. Restaurante Marisquería Córdoba.

Restaurante Marisquería Córdoba is a favorite among seafood aficionados. This restaurant specializes in fresh seafood, including lobster, grilled octopus, and a variety of fish cooked in traditional Spanish techniques. It's a great place for individuals looking for a genuine seafood experience since it's close to Benidorm's busy center.

Address: Avenida Alfonso Puchades, 8, Benidorm.
Price range: €30-50 per person.

Why tourists love it:

- Fresh and high-quality seafood.
- Authentic Spanish Dining Experience
- Ideal for seafood fans.

Benidorm's restaurant scene is dynamic, with a mix of traditional Spanish and foreign food. Whether travelers want a laid-back tapas bar, a romantic beach supper, or substantial British food, there is something for everyone.

Benidorm Travel Guide 2025

The numerous alternatives accommodate a wide variety of budgets, tastes, and dietary restrictions, making Benidorm an ideal trip for foodies.

Chapter 7

Local Crafts and Souvenirs

When visiting Benidorm, a busy coastal city known for its beaches and exciting nightlife, holidaymakers will definitely want to bring home souvenirs to remember their stay. Fortunately, Benidorm provides a diverse range of local crafts and souvenirs that highlight the region's rich culture and creative heritage. Everyone may find something for themselves, from classic Spanish things like pottery and leather goods to unique handmade jewelry and local culinary food. Here's a comprehensive reference of the greatest local crafts and souvenirs available in Benidorm.

1. Ceramics

Ceramics are one of the most popular souvenirs in Spain, and especially in Benidorm. Spain has a long tradition of manufacturing beautiful ceramics, and the Alicante area, which includes Benidorm, is well-known for its excellent pottery. Visitors will discover a diverse selection of handmade ceramic objects, including:

Traditional Spanish tiles, known as azulejos, are often painted with vibrant and ornate motifs. These tiles may serve as ornamental items, trivets, or coasters.

Bowls and plates: Hand-painted bowls and plates with vibrant designs are another popular option. These pieces make for distinctive kitchenware and make excellent presents for folks who appreciate cooking and serving Mediterranean-inspired cuisine.

Vases and Jugs: Ceramic vases and jugs come in a variety of sizes and shapes, and they often include traditional designs such as geometric patterns, floral themes, or even portrayals of local scenery.

Tourists may purchase ceramics at specialist stores around Benidorm as well as in Altea, a neighboring town known for its artisan crafts.

2. Leather goods

Spain is well-known for producing high-quality leather items, and Benidorm is no exception. Tourists may discover a variety of leather products, including:

Handbags: Spanish leather handbags are typically constructed of soft, durable leather and available in a range of styles, ranging from traditional to more modern.

Belts and wallets: Leather belts and wallets are attractive and useful mementos that may serve as long-term recollections of a visit to Benidorm. Many of these products are handmade, with delicate stitching and embossed embellishments.

Shoes and Sandals: Spanish leather shoes and sandals are readily accessible and well-known for their quality. The espadrille, a sandal constructed of canvas and rope, is a particularly famous Spanish item and an excellent summer accessory.

Benidorm's busy markets and shops provide a wide range of leather products, generally at moderate rates.

3. Jewelry

Handcrafted jewelry is another typical Benidorm souvenir. Visitors will discover a diverse collection of one-of-a-kind works, many of which are inspired by Spanish culture and environment. Some of the better possibilities are:

Silver Jewelry: Spain is well-known for its silver jewelry, and many local artists produce stunning necklaces, bracelets, and earrings with traditional Spanish motifs.

Mediterranean-Inspired Pieces: Some jewelry contains Mediterranean characteristics such as turquoise stones, coral, and seashells, making it ideal for souvenirs from a beach vacation in Benidorm.

Personalized Jewelry: Many local stores provide customized jewelry, enabling visitors to have their names or initials engraved on pendants or bracelets for a more personal keepsake.

For those looking for high-end, locally crafted jewelry, the adjacent city of Valencia has numerous outstanding artists and jewelers.

4. Textile and Embroidery

Handcrafted fabrics and embroidered products are excellent souvenirs from Benidorm. Many of these goods are created using ancient methods handed down through generations. Popular textile souvenirs include the following:

Tablecloths and Linens: Hand-embroidered tablecloths, napkins, and linens are sometimes embellished with elaborate motifs, making them attractive and distinctive presents.

Scarves and Shawls: Scarves and shawls made of high-quality textiles like silk, linen, or wool are widely available in Benidorm's markets. Some items use classic Spanish designs or floral themes.

Traditional Clothing: For a really unique keepsake, travelers may buy traditional Spanish apparel such as the mantilla (a lace or silk veil worn over the head and shoulders) or flamenco outfits, which are recognized for their vibrant colors and ruffled patterns.

5. Local Gourmet Products

Foodies will discover plenty of excellent local goods to take home as mementos. Benidorm and the surrounding area are noted for their high-quality gourmet items, which include:

Olive Oil: Spain is one of the world's leading producers of olive oil, and Spanish olive oil is renowned for its taste and quality. Tourists may purchase bottles of locally made olive oil, which are frequently packaged elegantly.

Wine: The Alicante area produces exceptional wines, including Monastrell reds and Moscatel dessert wines. Many local wine stores provide tastings, and guests may buy bottles to take home.

Turrón: This classic Spanish nougat prepared with almonds, honey, and sugar is a favorite delicacy, particularly during the holiday season. Jijona, near Benidorm, is well-known for making some of Spain's greatest turrón.

6. Handmade Fans

Traditional Spanish fans, or abanicos, are not only useful in the hot Mediterranean heat but also make a lovely and symbolic keepsake. These fans are generally hand-painted with complex motifs and are available in a range of colors and styles. Many stores in Benidorm sell handcrafted fans, and some even let clients see the artists at work.

7. Local Art & Paintings

Art fans can discover a wide range of locally made artwork in Benidorm's galleries and marketplaces. Some prominent alternatives are:

Watercolor Paintings: Local painters often make stunning watercolor paintings representing Benidorm's gorgeous scenery, including its beaches, ancient town, and surrounding mountains.

Sculptures and Carvings: Small sculptures and wooden carvings, often inspired by Spanish folklore or local fauna, are excellent ornamental mementos.

Street Art: Benidorm has a thriving street art culture, and visitors may buy reproductions of original works from local street artists, who often sell their work at fairs.

8. Flamenco Accessories

Flamenco is an iconic component of Spanish culture, and visitors to Benidorm may buy a range of flamenco-related things, including:

Flamenco Dresses: While a complete flamenco dress may not be an appropriate memento for everyone, smaller pieces such as ruffled scarves or ornamental accessories inspired by flamenco design are excellent memories.

Castanets: These percussion instruments are often utilized in flamenco performances. Castanets are available in a variety of sizes and shapes, and they make a distinctive and culturally valuable keepsake.

Popular Shopping Centers for Tourists

1. Centro Comercial La Marina

Centro Comercial La Marina, located just outside Benidorm in the adjoining town of Finestrat, is a popular retail complex among both residents and visitors. This spacious, contemporary mall has a diverse range of foreign and Spanish brands, making it an ideal location for anybody wishing to spend a full day shopping. Some of the main features of La Marina are:

Fashion retailers: Popular high-street labels include Zara, H&M, Bershka, and Pull & Bear, as well as designer retailers like Guess and Michael Kors. Whether you're searching for casual attire, formal dresses, or accessories, there is something for everyone.

The mall also contains a theater and an entertainment zone, making it ideal for families to visit.

Address: Avenida País Valencià 2, 03509 Finestrat.
Prices range from moderate to high-end.

2. Benidorm Indoor Market (Mercado Municipal).

The Benidorm Indoor Market is a must-see for travelers looking for a genuine local shopping experience. This lively market is a treasure trove of items and local products, providing a more traditional shopping experience than the contemporary malls. The indoor market, which is popular among both residents and visitors, is an excellent location to find:

Fresh Produce: If you want to try some local food, the market offers vendors offering fresh fruits, vegetables, meats, and cheeses. These are ideal for travelers living in self-catering hotels and wanting to prepare their own meals using genuine products.

Souvenirs & Handicrafts: The market also has a range of merchants offering one-of-a-kind souvenirs such as handmade products, leather goods, and traditional Spanish pottery. These one-of-a-kind items make great souvenirs for your vacation.

Address: Avenida de L'Aigüera, Benidorm
Price Range: Affordable.

3. Centro Comercial Plaza Mayor

The Centro Comercial Plaza Mayor is another well-known shopping attraction in Benidorm. While not as huge as La Marina, Plaza Mayor is centrally positioned in the city, making it readily accessible to visitors staying nearby. The mall provides a more relaxed shopping experience and features:

Fashion stores: Plaza Mayor, although not as large as La Marina, features a range of stores selling apparel, accessories, and footwear. Those wishing to freshen their wardrobes may choose from brands like Mango and Springfield.

Plaza Mayor is an excellent choice for travelers seeking a convenient area to conduct some casual shopping.

Address: Plaza Triangular, Benidorm
Price range: moderate.

4. Mercado Central (Central Market)

If you want to experience local culture while shopping, Mercado Central is the place to go. This colorful market not only sells local items but also provides an honest peek into the everyday lives of Benidorm locals. The highlights of the market include:

Local Food and Drink: Mercado Central is well-known for its variety of booths providing typical Spanish cuisine like cured meats, cheeses, and fresh seafood. You may also get local wines and olive oils, which are ideal for bringing a taste of Spain home.

Apparel and Accessories: Similar to the indoor market, Mercado Central contains merchants selling apparel, shoes, and accessories. Visitors will buy anything from casual summer clothing to traditional Spanish costumes. Mercado Central is a fantastic destination for travelers looking to enjoy traditional Spanish shopping while also purchasing unique gifts and local specialties.

Address: Calle Mercado, Benidorm.
Price Range: Affordable.

5. Carrefour shopping center

Centro Comercial Carrefour is a great option for vacationers searching for a one-stop store that sells everything from groceries to clothes and technology. While not precisely a shopping mall, Carrefour is a hypermarket that offers a diverse variety of items and services under one roof. Some of the important offers are:

Carrefour is perfect for guests living in self-catering flats since it allows them to stock up on food, cleaning supplies, and home products all in one handy place.

Electronics & Gadgets: Carrefour includes a department for gadgets, mobile phones, cameras, and other tech equipment.
Carrefour is situated outside of the city center, but it is readily accessible by bus or vehicle, making it a good alternative for those prepared to drive a little farther for their shopping.

Address: Avenida Comunidad Valenciana, Benidorm.
Price Range: Affordable.

6. Avenida Martinez Alejos Shopping Street

While not a standard retail mall, the Avenida de Martinez Alejos is one of Benidorm's most popular shopping areas. This pedestrian-friendly strip, along with a diverse range of stores and boutiques, is popular with travelers seeking a leisurely shopping experience. Highlights of shopping along this boulevard are:

Fashion Stores: Visitors may discover both worldwide brands and local businesses that sell apparel, shoes, and accessories. This is an excellent spot to get fashionable beachwear or evening wear for a night out in Benidorm.

Address: Avenida Martinez Alejos, Benidorm.
Price range: moderate.

Benidorm has a diverse range of shopping opportunities, from contemporary malls to historic markets and vibrant retail districts. Whether you're seeking worldwide fashion labels, one-of-a-kind souvenirs, or local cuisine items, one of the city's many shopping venues is likely to provide what you need.

Chapter 8

Nightlife Activities in Benidorm for Tourists

Benidorm is generally recognized as one of Spain's finest nightlife destinations, attracting visitors from all over the world who want to experience the exciting after-dark scene. Benidorm, known for its broad choice of clubs, pubs, live music venues, and entertainment acts, has something for everyone, whether you want to relax with drinks or party all night.

The city's nightlife is spread over many main districts, including the lively Levante Beach neighborhood, the famed "British Square," and the old town's more typical Spanish taverns and tapas restaurants.

1. Bar-hopping in the British Square

British Square, a popular nightlife destination in Benidorm, is noted for its bustling clubs, neon lights, and nonstop party atmosphere. As the name implies, many of the clubs and pubs in this area appeal to British visitors, with recognizable brands and music. However, the mood is worldwide, and people from all over the globe come to enjoy the festivities.

Morgan's Tavern: One of the most popular pubs in British Square, Morgan's Tavern is noted for its live entertainment, which includes tribute groups who play every night. This pub, known for its appearance on the TV program Benidorm, is ideal for a fun night out, with a stage for live music, themed evenings, and a dynamic audience.

Café Benidorm: Another must-see in British Square is Café Benidorm, which is a great place for late-night dancing. Known for its party atmosphere, this pub opens late and remains up until the early hours of the morning, playing a combination of commercial hits, party oldies, and live DJs.

The British Square is a terrific spot to start your night out, with lots of alternatives for bar-hopping before heading to the clubs later.

2. Clubbing on Levante Beach

Benidorm's Levante Beach is another popular nightlife destination, especially for those wishing to dance the night away at one of the city's many clubs. The seashore is dotted with pubs and nightclubs that appeal to a younger demographic, and the party often lasts into the early hours of the morning.

Penelope Disco: Penelope Disco is one of Benidorm's most renowned clubs, situated near Levante Beach and a must-see for electronic music fans. The club has a wide dance floor, many bars, and a VIP section. DJs play house, techno, and commercial dance music, and the club often stages themed evenings including international guest DJs.

KM Disco & Playa: This two-part venue has something for everyone. KM Playa, situated on the beachfront, is a terrific spot to start the night with cocktails and live music, while KM Disco is a big nightclub that keeps the party going until morning. With various dance floors, this club plays a wide range of music, including reggaeton, pop songs, and house music.

The Levante Beach neighborhood is ideal for travelers looking to enjoy the more vibrant side of Benidorm's nightlife, with lots of opportunities to dance and drink by the water.

3. Live Music and Cabaret Shows

Those who prefer live entertainment to partying can find a variety of places in Benidorm that provide live music, cabaret acts, and comedy performances. These places are ideal for travelers seeking a more relaxed, yet nonetheless exciting, night out.

Benidorm Palace: One of the city's most popular entertainment venues, Benidorm Palace hosts a range of acts such as cabaret, flamenco, and live music. The theater is famous for its lavish shows, which often include expensive costumes, acrobatics, and a blend of traditional and current Spanish music. The dinner-show experience is highly recommended for those seeking a full night of entertainment.

Rockstar Benidorm: If you like live music, here is the place to be. This renowned rock pub hosts live performances by local and international bands, ranging from classic rock to indie. The relaxed atmosphere and live performances make it a popular destination for music enthusiasts visiting the city.

Benidorm's live entertainment industry provides an excellent option for travelers seeking a fantastic night out without the intensity of the nightclub scene.

4. Tapas Bars and Local Cuisine in Old Town

For travelers searching for a more typical Spanish night out, Benidorm's old town has a variety of tapas pubs, and restaurants that provide a more relaxing and cultural ambiance. Spending the evening trying local food and drinking in a tapas bar is a classic Spanish experience, and Benidorm's old town provides the ideal setting.

Tapas Alley: For an authentic tapas experience, visit Benidorm's Tapas Alley, a short lane in the old town packed with tapas establishments serving a variety of small dishes. This is a terrific spot to go from pub to bar, sample new foods, and absorb the local vibe.

The old town is ideal for travelers looking to see true Spanish culture while enjoying wonderful cuisine and beverages in a more personal environment.

5. Gay-Friendly Nightlife in Benidorm

Benidorm is also recognized for its thriving and accepting LGBTQ+ nightlife scene, which includes various pubs and clubs dedicated to the homosexual community. The old town is home to a variety of gay-friendly establishments, including cabaret performances and dance parties.

Mercury Bar: One of Benidorm's most prominent gay pubs, Mercury Bar provides a warm and lively environment with frequent drag performances, themed evenings, and live music. The tavern is situated in the old town and is a popular hangout for both residents and visitors.

The Rich Bitch Show Bar: If you're looking for a night of humor and entertainment, this is the place to go. This pub is well-known for its entertaining drag acts, which combine humor, singing, and audience involvement to create a one-of-a-kind and amazing evening.

Benidorm's LGBTQ+ nightlife culture is diverse and dynamic, making it an appealing destination for all visitors.

6. Late Night Beach Bars

For those who wish to appreciate the beauty of Benidorm's beaches at night, the city has various late-night beach bars where you can unwind with a drink and enjoy the sea air. These pubs provide a more relaxed alternative to the clubs and are ideal for travelers looking to unwind after a full day of touring.

Daytona Rock Bar: Another popular beachside location, Daytona Rock Bar has live rock music and a laid-back atmosphere, making it an ideal spot to grab a drink and enjoy the evening air. The pub is situated on Levante Beach and is popular among both residents and visitors.

These beach bars provide a more relaxed approach to experiencing Benidorm's nightlife, enabling you to take in the city's natural beauty while enjoying a drink or two.

Benidorm Travel Guide 2025

Benidorm's nightlife is both diversified and exciting, with something for every sort of tourist. From the vibrant pubs and clubs of British Square and Levante Beach to the more traditional tapas restaurants and live music venues in the old town, there are limitless options for entertainment after dark.

Chapter 9

Itinerary Plan for Tourists in Benidorm.

Benidorm, on Spain's eastern Mediterranean coast, is known for its beautiful beaches, active nightlife, and a diverse range of activities for all sorts of tourists. Benidorm has everything, whether you want to relax, go on an adventure, or learn about culture. Here's a 7-day plan that will show you the finest of Benidorm.

Day 1: Arrival

Morning:

Arrival and check-in: Arrive in Benidorm and settle into your accommodations. Depending on your housing options, you may be staying in the popular Levante Beach area or the tranquil Poniente Beach sector.
Settle into your hotel: After your travel, spend some time to acquaint yourself with the hotel's services and surroundings.
Afternoon:

Levante Beach: Begin your Benidorm journey with a calm day at Levante Beach, one of the city's most popular destinations. Enjoy the golden beaches, crystal-clear waves, and breathtaking vistas of the Mediterranean Sea. Rent a sunbed, people-watch, and get a cool drink at a local seaside pub.

Evening:

Beachfront dinner: Visit a coastal restaurant for a fresh seafood meal with a view of the ocean. Many restaurants in the Levante Beach area provide delicious paella and tapas, ideal for your first supper in Benidorm.

Day 2: Explore Benidorm's Old Town.

Morning:

Old Town (Casco Antiguo): Spend the morning exploring Benidorm's attractive old town, which is famed for its small alleyways, typical Spanish architecture, and lively ambiance. Visit Plaza Mayor, the old town's center, and explore the local shops, cafés, and tapas restaurants.

Afternoon:

Visit the Church of San Jaime: Located in the old town, this 18th-century church is one of Benidorm's most famous attractions.

Explore the Old Town Market: Every Tuesday and Sunday, Benidorm's Old Town comes alive with a busy market. It's an excellent spot to buy local goods, souvenirs, and fresh fruit.

Evening:

Supper in Old Town: Relax with a leisurely supper at one of the charming tapas bars or small eateries in the Old Town. Try a range of tiny meals, including croquetas, patatas bravas, and jamón ibérico.

Day 3: Adventure at Terra Mítica Theme Park.

Morning:

On your third day in Benidorm, visit Terra Mítica, one of the region's top theme parks. Terra Mítica, located just outside the city, has portions inspired by ancient civilizations like Egypt, Greece, Rome, and Iberia. This is a must-see for adrenaline seekers and families alike. The park offers a range of roller coasters, water rides, and live entertainment.

Afternoon:

Afternoon activities at Terra Mítica include rides and themed sections. Don't miss the magnificent water displays and interactive exhibits that teach visitors about ancient civilizations.

Evening:

After a day of excitement at Terra Mítica, relax with a peaceful supper. For a tranquil supper with beach views, go to the Poniente Beach neighborhood, which is less touristy but still has plenty of superb eating choices.

Day 4: Day Trip to Guadalest

Morning:

Day excursion to Guadalest: Visit Guadalest, a lovely mountain hamlet situated only 30 minutes from Benidorm. This lovely community is noted for its medieval castle, breathtaking scenery, and the Guadalest Reservoir. Explore the history and displays of Guadalest Castle, which dates back to the 11th century.
Afternoon:

Explore the village: After seeing the castle, stroll around Guadalest's tiny alleyways, which are lined with art galleries, small museums, and charming stores offering local products.
Visit the Guadalest Reservoir: Don't miss the opportunity to photograph the turquoise waters surrounded by mountains.
Evening:

Return to Benidorm in the evening. If you have the energy, try a late-night drink at one of the bars on Levante Beach.

Day 5: Water sports and beaches.

Morning:

Water sports at Levante or Poniente Beach: On Day 5, engage in some daring activities. Jet skiing, parasailing, and windsurfing are among the water activities available at both Levante and Poniente beaches. There are several firms that provide rentals and instruction for both beginners and expert surfers.

Afternoon:

Beach relaxation: After a busy morning, spend the afternoon resting at the beach. Read a book, go swimming, or just enjoy the sunlight. You may also enjoy a stroll around Benidorm Marina.
Evening:

Beachfront eating and nightlife: Benidorm is well-known for its nightlife, so spend the evening enjoying a variety of supper and beverages. The neighborhood around British Square is noted for its vibrant taverns and entertainment. Try a beverage at Café Benidorm and take in the music scene.

Day 6: Visit the Terra Natura Zoo and Aqua Natura Water Park.

Morning:

Terra Natura Zoo: Spend the morning at Terra Natura Zoo, an innovative animal park located just outside Benidorm. The zoo is home to over 1,500 species and has immersive enclosures that mimic the animals' natural environments. Enjoy going around the park and seeing the animals, which include elephants, tigers, and giraffes.
Afternoon:

Aqua Natura Water Park: Located next to Terra Natura, the Aqua Natura Water Park is a terrific place to cool down after your zoo visit. Aqua Natura, with its water slides, wave pools, and peaceful lazy rivers, is an ideal place for families and anybody searching for water fun.
Evening:

Meal and a relaxed night: After a day of activity, unwind with a family-style meal.

Day 7: Shopping and Farewell to Benidorm

Morning:

Shopping at La Marina Shopping Center: On your last day, spend the morning in La Marina Shopping Center, which is situated on the outskirts of Benidorm. This retail mall has a variety of businesses, including fashion and electronics, as well as restaurants and cafés where you can get a snack.

Afternoon:

Poniente Beach is a calmer and more relaxing region than Levante, so spend the day recuperating there after a hard week. Take a walk along the promenade or just relax in the sun.

Evening:

Farewell meal: Wrap off your time in Benidorm with a farewell supper at a restaurant overlooking the Mediterranean Sea. Choose a location along the Levante Beach promenade for a last lunch of regional dishes like paella or arroz a banda.

Common Mistakes Tourists Should Avoid

1. Not planning for accommodation.

Mistake: Many travelers believe that they can just show up and get decent accommodations without any forethought. However, Benidorm is a popular resort all year round, particularly during peak seasons like summer and big holidays. As a consequence, hotels might become completely booked, and costs may rise during certain times.

Solution: Book your accommodations in advance, especially if you're going during busy tourist seasons. Consider your preferences—whether you want to stay near the beach, experience the busy nightlife, or choose a calmer spot. Booking.com and Airbnb provide a range of alternatives for various budgets and regions. Planning ahead of time may help you save money and prevent the stress of finding a place to stay at the last minute.

2. Underestimating the cost of dining out.

Error: While Benidorm is renowned for its low-cost dining alternatives, particularly for tourists, many visitors make the error of underestimating the expense of dining out, especially in tourist-heavy areas.

Solution: If you intend to eat at restaurants on the beach or near popular places such as Levante Beach, expect to pay more, particularly for cocktails. To minimize overpaying, go a bit farther inland, where you'll discover more genuine, affordable eateries. If you're staying in self-catering accommodation, you can purchase fresh goods from local markets like the Mercado Municipal and cook your meals, giving you a taste of Spanish cuisine while saving money.

3. Not using public transportation.

Mistake: Despite the fact that Benidorm's public transportation system is very simple to use, many visitors choose to use taxis or rent vehicles instead. This may be more costly and less convenient than taking the bus, tram, or walking.

Solution: Take use of Benidorm's tram system, which links the city to adjacent towns like Altea and Villajoyosa. It provides breathtaking coastline views and is an inexpensive and pleasant way to explore. Public buses are also a convenient method to move about town and are well-connected to major sites. The Tourist Card provides cheap transit for tourists, which is an excellent method to save money on transportation during your stay.

4. Ignore the weather forecast.

Mistake: Benidorm has a Mediterranean climate, with hot, dry summers and pleasant winters. Some travelers neglect to check the weather prediction, leaving them unprepared for unforeseen weather conditions.

Solution: Always check the weather prediction before traveling to Benidorm, and prepare appropriately. While sunscreen and lightweight clothes are vital throughout the year, a light jacket or sweater may be required in the colder months, particularly at night. Additionally, the summer heat may be extreme, so keeping hydrated and taking pauses in the shade are essential. In the winter and spring, expect intermittent rain showers.

5. Sticking to the tourist spots

Mistrake: Although Benidorm is well-known for its beaches and nightlife, many tourists make the error of focusing only on the big tourist attractions. This might lead to losing out on the city's many cultural offerings.

Solution: Go beyond the well-trodden route. Visit Benidorm's Old Town to see its original Spanish charm, small alleyways, and colorful buildings. For a more relaxing retreat, visit Elche Park or Cala Tio Ximo, a tiny, quiet beach. You might also go on a day excursion to neighboring towns like Altea or Guadalest, which have beautiful landscapes and historical buildings that will enhance your vacation experience.

6. Failing to budget for additional costs

Mistake: Tourists often ignore extra expenditures such as parking, tipping, or service taxes. For example, most restaurants in Spain charge a Servicio (service fee) or Cubierto (cover price) per guest, which may accumulate over time.

Solution: When eating out or attending tours, always ask if service costs are included. Furthermore, parking prices in Benidorm may be exorbitant in popular places, so consider parking choices in less congested regions of the city. Some hotels have free or cheap parking for visitors; ask about it when booking your reservation. Save some money for tips, since it is common to tip roughly 10% in restaurants and cafés.

7. Not using sunscreen and staying hydrated

Mistake: Benidorm is a sunny resort all year, and many people misjudge the sun's strength. Spending long hours on the beach or visiting the city without enough sun protection might result in sunburn and dehydration.

Solution: Always use a high-SPF sunscreen, even on overcast days, and reapply often, particularly after swimming. Furthermore, it is critical to keep hydrated during your journey, especially during the hotter months.

Carry a reusable water bottle and drink enough water to prevent heat-related ailments, which are often neglected in the excitement of a holiday.

Conclusion

Tourists may avoid these typical mistakes and have a more pleasurable vacation to Benidorm. A little planning may go a long way toward improving your trip, from arranging lodging and transportation to immersing yourself in local culture. Remember to take your time, remain hydrated, and enjoy all this colorful Spanish city has to offer.

Printed in Great Britain
by Amazon